Pamela Smith

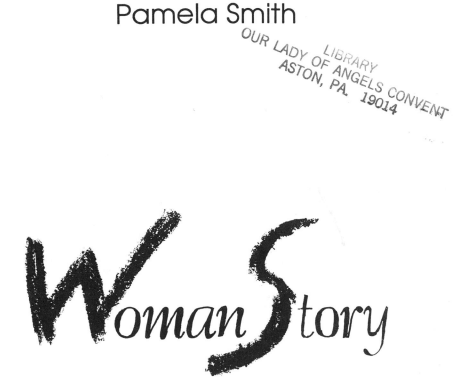

Woman Story

Biblical Models for Our Time

TWENTY-THIRD PUBLICATIONS
Mystic, Connecticut 06355

For the Rothenbergs
in memory of Julie

Art by Virginia DeWan, SS.C.M.

Twenty-Third Publications
185 Willow Street
P.O. Box 180
Mystic CT 06355
(203) 536-2611
800-321-0411

ISBN 0-89622-460-0
Library of Congress Catalog Card Number 91-71131

Excerpts from *The New Jerusalem Bible*, copyright © 1985 by Darton, Longman & Todd, Ltd. and Doubleday, a division of Bantam Doubleday Dell Publishing Group, Inc. Reprinted by permission.

Contents

INTRODUCTION

NEARLY 4000 YEARS of women, of feminine awareness, have shaped the heritage we call Judaeo-Christian. These reflections on the *anima*, the "womanspirit," of the Covenant are the body of my prayer. I hope that anyone who enters into them begins as I have: first of all, with Bible in hand. Then comes the re-imagining. And finally we move to the inward look, and the asking. There are several reasons, aside from the obvious current interest in women's religious experience, why I want to share these musings, sighs, and soul-songs now, with women and men.

Why?

Because at midlife I have had considerable experience with sin and more, I hope, with grace. Because I have met as much weakness as I have strength and have kept feeling that another strength, from elsewhere, persists and even intervenes.

Because, with the rest of the human race that bothers to notice these things, I have turned from ego to other and back again and have been knocked around by the echoing "I Am."

Because I feel that we, who are people of faith, are perhaps now more ready than ever to celebrate a wide, life-loving God who is male, female, both, neither, silent, boisterous, hidden, everywhere, and cannily finding us as our hearts awaken.

In offering this book to readers, I present it as I did to those who first perused it: as a gift to friends. The biblical passages, the second look at the stories, the prayers, and the questions for reflection have been the route into the consciousness, even the whole being, of the great women and the significant feminine images of the Old Testament. The friends and colleagues, male and female, who have shared these tell me that they have found it both helpful and intriguing to take a second look, day after day, in early morning or late evening, at the better known women of the pre-Christian story—Sarah, Deborah, Ruth, Hannah, Judith, and Esther, for example. But they have also mentioned their discovery of women who are noted but often overlooked as we read salvation history—women of import and impact like Hagar, Zipporah, Jephthah's daughter, Abigail, the widow of Zarephath, Azubah, the prophetess Huldah, the steadfast mother in Maccabees.

It has seemed important to me to look not only at triumphant women but at women who were taken for granted and never quite relieved of the frustrations and disappointment in their lives—like Jacob's wife Leah, or like so many women who ride city buses and push grocery carts in supermarkets every day. My increasing acquaintance with and awareness of the traumas of abused, molested women have given me a new light on Jacob's daughter Dinah, the concubine from Bethlehem (see page 32), and David's daughter Tamar. And women who have spilled out their distress over a son's or daughter's skewed values and destructive choices have clearly influenced how I have read (and thus portrayed) Hephzibah, the mother of violent, mad, and finally gentled Manasseh.

Beginning with the feminine aspect of the Creator and then spending time with the women of these told and retold stories also moves inevitably, it seems, into a new attention to the *animae* of the wisdom writings and the prophets. The creative genius of Wisdom ("she is a breath of the power of God"), the wavering and wayward yet glorious and graced figure of "Daughter Zion," the spirit of prayer, friendship, and peace have come at me, as I have looked more closely, with an earthiness and fecundity that is expressive of all women and of womanhood itself. Virgin, vineyard, bride of Yahweh, mother of peace are all *personae* which connect not only to the femininity of the Godhead but also with the cosmic maternity of the Jewish girl Mary.

As I have prayed, played with, pondered, and penned, a number of things have changed around in me (and I am, by the way, far from being a militant feminist). I hope that the reader's perceptions and appreciations of the Godliness of women and the wom-

2

anliness of God are at least assisted, if not changed, by these chapters. They are meant for Christian women, whether Catholic or Quaker; for men, whether patriarchal or altogether brotherly and capable of balanced partnerships (as my own brothers are); for the sons and daughters of Abraham, whether Jewish or Moslem; for anyone who simply finds them interesting.

I hope that my jottings will be read by individuals who wish to dig more deeply into a vast faith tradition, and perhaps even by groups who wish to break open the Word together. Above all, I hope that these meditative pieces are read, as I mentioned before, by *friends,* in a cross-cultural and inter-religious sense—by friends with the piety and reverence of Hasids, the mystic gentleness of Sufis, the patient time of Christian and Buddhist monastics, the harmony with all that is which exists within anyone and all who have the touch of the contemplative...if only for a few moments a day.

THE PLAYFUL MAKER OF GENESIS

(Read Genesis 1:1–2:4)

God saw all (s)he had made, and indeed it was very good. Genesis 1:31

THE STRONG and all-holy One gazed across a lonely night and realized something, out of nothing.

She scooped thin air in wisps and bundles to her heart. She held it close as her heart beat gently, assuredly, large with love. And they were born: nova, supernova, galaxy, nebula, meteorite, black hole, planet, sun. They exploded, were flung with joy, and spun. Then, in a deliberate, warm passion she clasped a mass in her hands. She rounded it, worked it, molded it—warm. And it became earth. As she fondled it and held it to her breasts, more were born: land, stone, mountain, cactus, tree, salamander, bird, bobcat, grapevine, jungle, wheatfield, man, woman, and the thousands of living wonders their eyes looked on.

The rivers that rose, the oceans, the lakes, the pools and puddles and streams were caresses and kisses she could never stop giving to all she had called into being. They shrank and swelled with the rhythm of moon, the echo of pulse and heartsound.

The more that she loved, the more comets and African violets and curly-haired people who made up words and danced and sang songs there were.

It was good. They all were.

All that they needed was to remember...to listen for the beat of the heart—under, above, within them all—and to know the body, the One, who waved, called home, embraced, pressed together, held tight. And set free. To celebrate. To live—loose, bonded, light, dark, amazingly different, simple, multiform, pure, true, wild, bizarre. And the same as everything.

So, God, I begin with an "O!"—reverently.

QUESTIONS FOR REFLECTION AND DISCUSSION

• The idea of a God who laughs and plays and delights in earthly things strikes many believers as a novelty, if not a near-heresy. What evidence in Scripture and what testimony in the lives of holy people can assure us that we worship a playful, lavish God?

• Feminist theological and spiritual writing of recent years has done much to awaken us to an image of God as birth-mother and to call attention to the nurturing attributes of the Creator. Does a presentation of God as a feminine Creator contradict the notion of a fatherly God, supplant it, or complement that image for you? Why?

• Eco-theologians like Thomas Berry (author of *Befriending the Earth*, Twenty-Third Publications, 1991) have called us to a reverence for the planet and for all creation in an altogether new way. Peter Russell (creator of the video *The Global Brain*) highlights the new scientific and spiritual perception of the earth as a "single living organism." What, in your own spiritual experience or your own long thoughts, tunes you in to a sense of the essential unity of all creation?

Eve, the Mother of Confusion
(Read Genesis 2:18–3:24)

Then the snake said to the woman, "No! You will not die! God knows in fact that the day you eat it your eyes will be opened and you will be like gods, knowing good from evil." The woman saw that the tree was good to eat and pleasing to the eye, and that it was enticing for the wisdom that it could give. Genesis 3:4–6

SOMETHING TURNED on its head. Something slithered out of a shrub. Something bit into her thoughts.

She began to name this night rain "bad," that dewfall "good," this thunder "enemy," that cloudbreak "friend." She began to be afraid of the man she had twinned with because she knew that, no matter what, she could never completely hold him. And she felt more and more unknown. Later her daughters and sons would call that first split of the mind "temptation." They would call her decision to try to understand everything on her own "sin."

It was not so easy to dance when one became deaf to the cosmic rhythm. It was less so when harmonies became amnesia and the memories of dissonance lingered on.

She wondered if it were too late to hope that whatever had sidled into her garden and twisted idea into tightly coiled delusion could somehow be trampled down.

Maybe.

God, unchain my mind, let music ring, and set my feet free. I need.

Questions for Reflection and Discussion

• Basic to the nature of human sin is the yen to have it all, know it all, control, be a god-unto-oneself. Does the sin of Adam and Eve resonate with your own experience of sin?

• Alienation, separation, and disjunction are not the only aspects and consequences of sin. Another seems to be the temptation to lose hope, to fear that recovery is an impossibility. When do you find yourself most sorely tempted to abandon hope? What brings you back?

SARAH THE BARREN
(Read Genesis 15–18; 20–22)

Abraham was a hundred years old when his son Isaac was born to him. Sarah said: "God has given me cause to laugh! All who hear about this will laugh with me!" Genesis 21:5–6

THE BARREN WOMAN wanted the proxy son, shared a man for him, and then did not want the boy after all. Ishmael. The child tugged this way and that, tugged hard, for home. He was surrogate, step-chiid, adoption, refusal, slave boy, bowman. And meant to be a patriarch in his own way. He lived, despite the barren woman's uncaring and improvident goodbye. The barren woman wanted her own child and then scoffed at the absurdity. Isaac. She tittered, cackled, brushed away and off, but then fell quiet when she grew and felt life stir. He was the son of her life-longing, the child promised to father sand and stars. She cried desert springs, surprising, out of rocks. She cried night rain. And she laughed at the joke which God had played.

Her divided heart never entirely healed. An excess of jealousy or hurt or rage distanced Ishmael forever. In hardness, she abandoned him. An excess of desire and delight and stupefaction held Isaac as her only love. Abraham? He was there, the latter-day father, ambivalent husband, a sometimes edgy one who could trade her off as his sister. He was the eager host of men with prophecies by a terebinth in Mamre, the wondrous rescuing uncle. He was great-souled, faithful, and a fuddy-duddy. He was a generally, but not entirely, good man who finally listened.

She was a good wife for him.

God worked a whole history through their possibly few moments of attention and clarity. The rest? God seemed to let their errors and their dull-witted days be. God shrugged so much of it away, chuckling, "Yitsaq, Yitsaq, Yitsaq," even as water was lovingly drawn for thirsty Ishmael. Even as a ram got stuck in the thicket on Isaac Hill.

God, turn my ineptness into your good will, my dismaying laughter into your indulgent smile, my roughness and my wrinkles into your soft smoothing.

QUESTIONS FOR REFLECTION AND DISCUSSION

• In some notable ways, Sarah fits the unfortunate stereotype of women as fickle and unpredictable. Abraham, however, also fits that description at moments. How do you account for the fact that the divine design depended so much on two unlikely people who clearly did not always "have it all together"? What does that say to you about yourself?

• The birth of Isaac comes across to us simultaneously as miraculous intervention and a colossal practical joke. Can you relate any divine surprises in your life that suggest that God has a sense of irony and humor?

HAGAR THE SLAVE
(Read Genesis 16:1–15; 21:9–21)

Hagar gave a name to Yahweh who had spoken to her, "You are El Roi," by which she meant, "Did I not go on seeing here, after him who sees me?" This is why the well is called the well of Lahai Roi.... Genesis 16:13–14

SHE LISTENED TO GOD, and so did Abraham. God heard her too. The one who was listening only to the desperation and then the jealousy, the hurt, the overprotective greed of her own heart was Sarah. Hagar and Abraham heard God even as they received Sarah's unreason and mistreatment. They were given a promise.

Part of the promise brought her a spring in the wilderness as her crying boy sat under a shrub. Part of the promise brought her an archer, a wild, sun-toughened warrior. Part of the promise brought a wife out of Egypt for her son. And so her grandchildren, after the centuries and millennia of descents, are today the people of surrender, the people of prayer and fast and alms and pilgrimage, the people of the creed: for One. Islam. Allah, also God, was Hagar's "God of Vision." The slave who was set free— or, more exactly, turned loose resourcelessly—saw. She lived. She believed. Her eyes opened wider, opened to water in the desert, to hope.

But she had not heard or seen everything. A snatch. A glimpse. She had seen God, and then a grown man with arrows. There were no minarets in sight as she set out on hegira without her destination named, as she made Ramadan but could only thirst blankly, as she gave away the alms of her security.

God, help me to go ahead without having to see the end—or the sense— of my wayfaring.

QUESTIONS FOR REFLECTION AND DISCUSSION

- A theme in the life of Hagar is the sustaining power of her vision, especially her view of God. What is your own vision of God? How, during times of conflict with others, have you observed that God was seeing you through?
- There are many points of common faith among Moslems, Jews, and Christians. The descendants of Abraham and Hagar, the descendants of Ishmael, are often connected with the Moslem faith. Can you relate how the "five pillars of Islam" (proclaiming belief in one God, prayer, fasting, almsgiving, and pilgrimage) relate to the mainstays of your own faith?

REBEKAH OF SPRING

(Read Genesis 24)

She went down to the spring, filled her pitcher, and came up again. Running towards her, the servant said, "Please give me a sip of water from your pitcher." She replied, "Drink, my lord...I will draw water for your camels, too, until they have had enough." Genesis 24:16–19

REBEKAH WAS the unearthly beauty who was ready for anything, the soul of surprise welcomed, the once-virgin mother of hospitality.

She was not the first, and certainly not the last, among women who met life-altering strangers at springs or wells. She was not the first, and certainly not the last, among water-gatherers who filled empty jugs and then spilled out their own precious water for men, for children, for camels. She believed that thirst was to be quenched, and she was glad to give herself over to the quenching.

Rebekah wore gold—a ring in her nose, wide bracelets. She was a woman who could gladly receive gifts, let others lay claims on her, and set out for another country. She was fine mettle.

Home was where she brought people. Home was a place she carried with her, making room for everyone wherever she would go. Home was the invisible embrace she gave with her friendly words, her gracious giving. Home was the blessing she bore along for all, for the one standing in the field whom she had been awaiting and guessing at a distance.

Rebekah was like a spring herself, deep running, spilling across face and hands, ready to be drunk in, circling in a slow, fluid ring, yes and yes, and yes again.

God, give me the grace of the jug-bearer, a heart that is shelter and resting place, a life-gift to pour out that is myself and more. Give me your good watercourse to waken and swim in, to be aswirl with, to spill over on someone's great thirst. Is it much that I ask, O Living Water?

QUESTIONS FOR REFLECTION AND DISCUSSION

• In Christian monastic spirituality, the charism, even the vow, of hospitality gets significant emphasis. The spirit of Rebekah seems imbued with a "hospitality of the heart" which welcomes the stranger and the guest and makes every place "home." Where have you experienced this type of hospitality, and where (and to whom) do you find yourself particularly called to offer it?

• The image of water—"living," flowing, quenching water—is an important one in the Old and the New Testaments. What does water suggest and symbolize to you? How does it relate to your own experience of God? Has water ever played a real or symbolic role in setting your direction for the future?

LEAH THE LOVELORN
(Read Genesis 29-30)

When Yahweh saw that Leah was unloved, he opened her womb, while Rachel remained barren. Genesis 29:31

IT CAN BE MADNESS and torture to be next-best, even if one is first-best at childbearing.

She knew that she was a trick, a pawn, the second-string, a booby prize. She knew that she had a husband who played roulette wheels with women, wives, and maidservants, and had joy, if from nothing else, in having sons. She gave him sons. She gave him Zilpah to have more sons, in her name. Then she also had more sons. She gave him a daughter.

Her husband was a fooled man who had long been a master of deception and impostering.

Leah was a wife who fooled no one, once morning came. And she was used. She gave herself over to an unhappy place. And she probably never knew what being cherished for herself, what having a man devotedly in love with her, could be.

Her meaning? The children.

In spite of the workaday life of tents, food, fields, babies, and lying still at night wondering what woman her man would choose, she loved her children. Her sons became rough-and-tumble strong men.

And she came to know the God of Jacob, the God who wrestled with him and won, for she knew what it was to wrestle—and not to perceive the end. What followed the contests? Tribes upon tribes of scholars, merchants, innkeepers, rabbis, wise women and wise men, ambassadors, kings, writers, producers, directors, economists, nurses, doctors, scientists, philosophers, and healers of troubled souls and minds. Her children and her children's children persisted. They flourished, spread, suffered, moved, founded, died in prison and pogroms and gas, rose again, built their nation with her husband's name: Israel. The children of her fertility blossomed, burgeoned, hosannaed...though Leah herself had hardly been loved.

Perhaps for her the offspring and aftermath were, indeed, enough.

God, make me fertile—creative, nurturing, enduring, future-filled, even when I fear no one is particularly fond of me. Help me live for the more, the other, the next, and let them continue far beyond me. You are the God of growth and centuries.

QUESTIONS FOR REFLECTION AND DISCUSSION

• Like Hagar, Leah could not have dreamed of the immense role she has played in millennia of religious history. She was the ancestor of countless Jewish people of brilliant achievement. Christians claim her as a foremother of Jesus. In your own family history, can you identify people who had a profoundly influential role, who started or built something which far surpassed their dreams? As you remember them, consider how the "hand of God" was at work in their life stories.

• Leah is a kind of archetype of the unloved and under-appreciated woman. Among people you have known, what would you say become the rewards or consolations for those whose lives have made a great difference, even though they themselves were taken for granted or underrated?

RACHEL, LATE MATRIARCH

(Read Genesis 29–31; 35:1–20)

Leah had lovely eyes, but Rachel was shapely and beautiful, and Jacob had fallen in love with Rachel....So Jacob worked for seven years for Rachel, and they seemed to him like a few days because he loved her so much. Genesis 29:17, 20

LIKE A STAIRCASE to heaven dancing with glad and gift-bundled angels, she was the object of Jacob's desire and dreaming.

Rachel must have been astonishing—the kind of woman who set a man's heart beating till he thought it would explode through the skin of his chest, the kind of woman who flattened a man out so that he would wait and wait, crawling. Fourteen years as an indentured servant to his uncle Laban didn't seem too much for lovestruck Jacob.

And she? She suffered his love and her infertility and their frustration and his outbursts of propagating with her sister and two maidservants. As Jacob had for her, Rachel waited.

She waited for the son Joseph, who later was nearly the death of him, the father who loved too fondly and much. She waited for the son Benjamin, who was, in labor, the death of her.

Along the way she picked up some of her husband's tricks.

The beautiful body of Rachel bore.

The beautiful heart of Rachel gave herself, gave up, gave over. The beautiful mind of Rachel reasoned how to steal away her father's idols, and steal she did, successfully. She never did learn, however, how to carry off her husband's idols. They were perhaps more subtle and locked inside, deadbolted in his occasional spasms of pride. Most importantly, though, the beautiful spirit of Rachel understood where God's spirit was leading next, after twenty years of Jacob in her father's land. And she encouraged and traveled with him into that next. She, the fair and far-waiting, moved, aha and okay, into the next real phase of dreaming Israel.

God, if you give me nothing else, give me a Joseph, a spirit-child, a God-son, who will prosper and forgive and take the ones who would hurt him into his arms. Give me that kind of beauty. And give me a readiness for the new—to survive and pass on.

QUESTIONS FOR REFLECTION AND DISCUSSION

• Beautiful, beloved, and long pained by childlessness—that was the lot of Rachel. Identify the "childlessness" in your own life—actual childlessness or some unfulfillment which has saddened you. Then reflect on what you have learned and even gained from that experience of emptiness.

• Religious history and the personal spiritual journey often involve prolonged periods of waiting. Where have you experienced a long wait for something and realized that the wait resulted in something far better than you originally hoped for?

DINAH ALONE

(Read Genesis 34)

Simeon and Levi, Dinah's brothers, each took his sword and advanced unopposed against the town and slaughtered all the males. They killed Hamor and his son Shechem with the sword, removed Dinah from Shechem's house, and came away. When Jacob's other sons came on the slain, they pillaged the town in reprisal for the dishonoring of their sister. Genesis 34:25–27

DINAH WAS THE MATRIARCH of the thirteenth tribe of Israel, a tribe of particular women: the centuries-long—and old as humanity—tribe of abused, molested, raped, and stolen women.

There was not yet for her a Jesus, a nailed man, who could help her feel that God would understand what it was to be taken and slammed into. Dinah knew neither gods nor men who seemed able to plumb helplessness and wrench something holy and free from that nothing.

She did know brothers and their anger and revenge. She did know that some men could take and then pay if other men became angry enough to believe that something had been taken from THEM.

Nobody stayed with Dinah to find exactly what had been taken from HER.

Not yet.

She was the mother of a tribe of ravaged and ransacked women who were never questioned about their loss, never asked if anything was left of them.

She was cleaned up, carried home, and made the cause of a sword trick and murder and shouting. No one noticed that her soul still lay there on that spot of ground. No one cared to listen to the undersounds of the unspeakable.

She was queen mother of the tribe of women who had need of soft and slow restoring. But no one heard her booming silence then.

No one yet.

Lord, I pray for the dumbstruck women, the women who have stayed in some sad and fearful place, the women who have never given voice to their outrage and screaming. I want to walk with them and give ear to their great quiet. And help to their rebuilding. I want to mention you, a God violently made victim...a soft, hurt God who comes back strong.

QUESTIONS FOR REFLECTION AND DISCUSSION

• What is there to say about victims of violence and violation? There is only the question to ask: What can we do to help restore them? What personal initiatives and what moves in society might we make to assist their healing?

Tamar's Line

(Read Genesis 38)

Judah, seeing her, took her for a prostitute, since her face was veiled. Going up to her on the road, he said, "Here, let me sleep with you." Genesis 38:15–16

FROM PEREZ: Boaz, Obed, Jesse, David the king, Solomon, and, a long way down, the Messiah. All from the line of Judah.

Tamar was a woman of some character or no character, depending on the optics and judgment of the seer. She was invisible and may well have been blind-folded like Dame Justice, with scales in her hands, the day she waited by the roadside aping the whore. Her sense of rightness and justice told her that she deserved sons related somehow to her bygone husband, Er. She was compelled to explore and exhaust every possibility in a land where lineage and the name of the father were what lasted, what lived on.

Onan had failed her coming and going. Her father-in-law cheated her out of the next one, Shelah. And so the old man himself did not repulse her as long as she thought of fair play, connection, family, sons who needed a heritage, a rooted tree.

It was the children one lived for, no matter what darkness they came from. No matter that their father could have been their grandfather, was myopic, and fell upon his fathering one listless and lust-rusty day when he was left alone and had a goat to pay. She had won: a life that would last, twin children, and the name. Tamar barely blinked as she played out this woman's game, laid down the inner law, got her just deserts, and turned a dirty joke into the whole world's holy fate.

God, may my compulsions and my wantings work to your purposes, whether or not I know or see, whether or not I sin or succeed.

Questions for Reflection and Discussion

• In the letter to the Romans, St. Paul speaks of "all things working toward the good" for those who love God. That is not the same as justifying a corrupt, skewed means by a worthy purpose or end. It is, however, a statement of faith that God can make good on anything. Where do you see this in the story of Tamar? Where have you seen it in the lives of people you know?

• Tamar, typical of the women of her time and ages after, was convinced of the importance of name and family line. Why, in the Christian era, do you suppose that raising up physical descendants and continuing the family name has received less and less emphasis?

Asenath

(Read Genesis 41:43–57)

Pharaoh named Joseph Zaphenath-Paneah, and gave him Asenath daughter of Potiphera, priest of On, to be his wife. And Joseph began to journey all over Egypt. Genesis 41:45

OUT OF EGYPT God called Asenath.

Her man was a dreamer and seer, a man of hope and destiny, a man of foresight and planning, a man who had visions of truth and famine and self and stewarding.

For a long while no one much cared when or whether or whom Asenath mothered. It was the man she married that they watched. Old stories said he had been sold and slandered and that he had smiled through prison. They knew of his foreknowledge and wisdom. They suspected he had secrets and perhaps sacred strengths.

God called Asenath remarkable and worthy. She was match for a wronged man who had forgiven, a favored man who gave worlds away, a powerful man who wept for his poor envious family. Joseph, in his own time and in his coat of multi-memory, was a redeemer. And Asenath was one with him.

Bless, O Lord, those with whom we link ourselves, and best us with and to each other. Best us, Lord, in you.

Questions for Reflection and Discussion

• Joseph, of course, is the star of the Joseph story, and he is often seen as a prototype of the Messiah. What sort of woman would one have to be to live and grow with the gentle, altruistic, saintly type? How do couples whose intimacy includes a very deep shared spirituality get to be that way?

Young Miriam

(Read Exodus 2:1–10; 15:1–21; Numbers 12:9–15)

The child's sister then said to Pharaoh's daughter, "Shall I go and find you a nurse among the Hebrew women to nurse the child for you?" "Yes," said Pharaoh's daughter, and the girl went and called the child's own mother. Exodus 2:7–8

IT MATTERS LESS that she nearly ended a leper than that she began in water.

She loved the born child and, as she watched amid the reeds, her only thought was to save.

Life was Miriam's first law.

Lord, let me go to lengths—wade into water, hide in deep bulrushes, lead the joyous with crazed tambourines—just, just for all who live.

QUESTIONS FOR REFLECTION AND DISCUSSION

• Miriam and her mother went to extremes to save the life of Moses. What actions on behalf of life do you consider appropriate, even though they might be deemed "extreme"? How have you personally felt called to be involved in pro-life (or pro-peace or pro-people) causes?

• The parents and family of Moses had to give up something tremendous in order to save him: his "belonging" to them. What sacrifices have you had to make, or do you anticipate having to make, in order to serve a greater good and/or someone's well-being?

ZIPPORAH, THE WOMAN FOR MOSES

(Read Exodus 2:16–3:14)

When they returned to their father, Reuel, he said to them, "Why are you back so early today?" "An Egyptian protected us from the shepherds," they said, "and he even drew water for us and watered the flock." "And where is he?" he asked his daughters. "Why did you leave the man there? Ask him to eat with us." Moses agreed to stay on there with the man, who gave him his daughter Zipporah in marriage. Exodus 2:18–21

SHE TOOK HIM IN, the tall stranger with his runaway pain and ready rescuing, as easily as she called the rag-tag tufted flock and six simple sisters.

Long before their plain wedding and tented dusks, she had flashed with mountain burnings. She felt something else, away, farther than thunder, something that crackled in her, lightning and sparks, but ate up nothing. At times she thought that quick flame was someone, though she hadn't met him. He kept escaping, faster and more flickering than fireflies. But yet she drew, like chill hands to hot coals, awed and expectant, to the night sky and the horizon line.

That was before, long before, the desert and the daystar's cloud or sleep's dark fire.

She was light.

She began to circle outside time with this eerily familiar Moses, the saving stranger, the one to be God's stone and serpent man. She bore, all at once, the future and the past: Gershom and Joseph's bones. She had been ready all along to burst into camplight and hearth fire and funeral pyre. She too had stood on holy ground and felt something warm and mountainous before her. But she could not breathe a name.

The first night she dozed with Moses and their breathing started and dropped together, she recognized the breath of God. Moses and all of it fanned that distant, lasting flame. And breathed and breathed and breathed it up.

Lord, sometimes I am sure that you and I met before I was born, but then it was nearly all forgotten. And then I meet some striking person. I say to myself: This one, certainly, is of God. And another comes. I think: And so is this one. I smell a waft of smoke, and I am ready again for caravans of those who have known you, here and there, in earth's deep and in the farthest bright-hot star. I breathe in again.

QUESTIONS FOR REFLECTION AND DISCUSSION

• When we love someone who seems to have a special call, a unique destiny, about him or her, our active and present loving must be delicately balanced with a letting-go. Moses' wife Zipporah certainly knew that. Where in your life have you had to "let go" of someone so that she or he would be more free to pursue a vision or follow a dream?

• There do seem to be persons who are "made for each other," whether as friends or as married lovers. How do you account for the kind of bonding which seems to allow people to see through to one another's souls? And how do you nourish a spiritual love so that it continues to grow?

WOMAN OF VISION:
THE SPIRIT OF EXODUS

(Read Exodus 17:1–7 and Deuteronomy 33:8)

Yahweh then said to Moses...."Strike the rock, and water will come out for the people to drink." Exodus 17:5,7

AS SHE BENT OVER the walking water of the windlicked pool, she paused, transfixed. She saw her face, the Red Sea parting, and someone drenching in the latterday Jordan. They were sudden and very much the same: her own and millions of visages that woke in the circling waves and went out, adding, adding.

There was someone who would explode from water, and they would wash and cloudburst, cloudburst ever after. New pools would form, new faces wake. And they would wash, and they would cloudburst. And newer pools would form. And newer faces would wake. And they would wash. And they would cloudburst. They would splash, they'd new pool and new, new face and wash and wake. And wake. And wake.

Someone was drenching in the latterday Jordan.

They were sudden and very much the same, those who would wake and wake.

O God, we are more than ourselves...and, with you, so much farther.

QUESTIONS FOR REFLECTION AND DISCUSSION

• The River Jordan has been a river of destiny in its crossing into the Promised Land and in the baptism of Jesus. Imagine yourself looking fixedly into its waters. What would you see there? And what future might you imagine?

• The "spirit of Exodus" in this mini-chapter is, of course, not a specific woman but instead a spiritual reality which we might simply call a "sense of history." How is a sense of history important in your own spiritual life and in your religious affiliation? How is that sense of history periodically reawakened for you?

RAHAB OF JERICHO
(Read Joshua 2; 6:17–25)

The two men had not yet settled down for the night when Rahab came up to them on the roof. She said to them, "I know that Yahweh has given you this country...." Joshua 2:8–9

SHE WAS THE TYPE, they surmised, who would let anyone in for favor or pay. She was also the type who felt the Jericho fear: the fear of a God who could do anything in or under the heavens. And so this fear, with the first fragments of faith, made her friendly. She gave flaxen hiding places, rope ladders, and advice. She won a scarlet cord and a home in the Promised Land she had just begun to hear of.

So much for old habits made more of.

Lord, help me to perceive and welcome the present opportunity. Help me to be pulled willingly into events and actions which are larger and more lasting than my past.

QUESTIONS FOR REFLECTION AND DISCUSSION

• It is already a kind of religious cliché to say that the greatest sinners make the greatest saints. Rahab is an early example of that phenomenon. What do you suppose causes someone whose life has been unspectacular and even sinful suddenly to "rise to the occasion," to take a tremendous risk, to make a "leap of faith," and to be changed forever after?

• Why do you suppose that Matthew makes it a point to mention in his genealogy of Jesus (Matthew 1:1–17) several less-than-ideal ancestors, including Tamar and Rahab?

DEBORAH THE JUDGE
(Read Judges 4-5)

They sang a song that day, Deborah and Barak, son of Abinoam, and the words were: "That the warriors in Israel unbound their hair, that the people came forward with a will, bless Yahweh!" Judges 5:1–2

DEBORAH AROSE after a left-handed judge amid Israel's offenses and palm trees. She bore neither a foot-long blade nor a battling oxgoad. She did, however, carry Barak and a people. After mayhem, since she believed in the outcome, she was able to sing a song.

Deborah was one who took on a destiny and made war at Mt. Tabor. Hardly ready to be transfigured, she could, however, take history—and apparent inevitability—and, in part, reshape it. She routed hopeless new gods and the robbers of freedom.

With that, and sad blood, she made her canticles.

Deborah, my Lord, was the first of Israel's acknowledged women leaders. Though ruthless and expedient, she, like so many less-than-heartrich, rescued your people and gave them rest. Help me, O Wisdom, to be tough where you want it, yet tender, too.

QUESTIONS FOR REFLECTION AND DISCUSSION

• Both Deborah and Jael (see Judges 4:17–22) were women of God who dealt with an enemy violently. Deborah's canticle praises God for the destruction of Sisera and implores continued triumph. At this point in our spiritual history, what do you perceive to be the role of women in times of violent conflict? What do you see as the appropriate Christian response to violence in general?

THE DAUGHTER WHO
PLAYED TAMBOURINES AND DANCED
(Read Judges 11)

When he saw her, he tore his clothes and exclaimed, "Oh my daughter, what misery you have brought upon me!....I have made a promise before Yahweh which I cannot retract." Judges 11:35

THE NAME OF JEPHTHAH'S daughter might just as well have been Marah. For some, the most curious thing was that she took her girlfriends and handmaids away and mourned her virginity.

For others, the oddest thing was that she assented, without fuss, to a wild, ungodly promise: to be a human sacrifice.

Unlike the mountain scene with Abraham and Isaac, no angel came to stay the father's hand. No sheep caught in the bush got rushed, thumping and hoof twitching, into her place. She bled. But before that she let her sorrow be known: that she had had no lover, no children. That was all, she may have thought, a woman might ask. She never wondered, as she settled onto the altar of a strange vow, whether the man who gave away her life might be mistaken.

The left women, then and thereafter, mourned with her and for her, some days each year: four.

Dear God, let me know when to be silent and when to speak, when to protest and when to accept, when to go along respectfully and when to flee. Let me not end mourning but faithful to the truer you...and free.

QUESTIONS FOR REFLECTION AND DISCUSSION

• Jephthah's daughter was the victim of a poorly discerned, impulsive promise. What are the indicators that a promise needs reconsidering? What are the signs in discernment that a movement or decision is really of God?

THE WIFE OF MANOAH

(Read Judges 13–16)

The Angel of Yahweh appeared to this woman and said to her, "You are barren and have had no child, but you are going to conceive and give birth to a son. From now on, take great care. Drink no wine or fermented liquor, and eat nothing unclean....No razor is to touch his head, for the boy is to be God's nazirite from his mother's womb; and he will start rescuing Israel from the power of the Philistines." Judges 13:3–5

WHILE DELILAH PROVED a fatal charm, while a harlot had softened him long before he pulled apart Gaza, while his wife had been traded away to his best man, Samson at least had the consolation that he still had a mother.

Of all the women, she seemed the only faithful one. She had waited, prayed, reviewed, obeyed. She and Manoah staked their lives on angels, mysterious names, and the God unknown.

It was hard to square his consecrated strength with his mad behavior—tail-tied foxes, jawbones, and the earthquake that was Samson felling the temple of Dagon. The only sense that came of it was the clearing of the land, the drubbing of the Philistines like burned-down trees, plowed-under weed stubble, and chucked stones. She wondered at his wildfire.

But his mother could appreciate a safe place for farming and settling a home.

God, give me a precious one who holds his own; give me a darling who eases the hurt and squelches harm's trickster; give me youths who come true and secure; give me a people all healed of their anger. Will you muster up a better?

QUESTIONS FOR REFLECTION AND DISCUSSION

• The story of Samson is a strange mixture of history and superstition. Where, in the story of Manoah and his wife, do you find simple, uncomplicated faith?

• Whatever the morality or lack of it in Samson's violence, what respectable purposes are served? How do you account for the Old Testament's portrayal of Samson as a foolish hero?

THE WOMEN,
AFTER THE HORROR AT GIBEAH

(Read Judges 19-21)

In the morning her husband got up and, opening the door of the house, was going out to continue his journey when he saw the woman, his concubine, lying at the door of the house with her hands on the threshold. "Get up," he said, "we must leave!" There was no answer. Judges 19:27–28

IT HAS A LONG, ugly history, the brutal and frenzied gang rape. The collapsed concubine who had been used all night and then was cut to pieces was nameless. But she had a name: Woman. Woman, as defined by the heartless. Woman, as kept by the property keepers. Woman, as pierced and battered and rammed and killed by those who see no one, sense nothing but their drunken appetite and the turn-on of blood, feel nowhere but for holes in rocks.

After the concubine there were other women, some violated, some shamed by the thought, all sisters. While many died, there were those who survived. They wanted to speak about heartbeats. They wanted to remember exhaustion and pain. They were angry. And silent. And stupefied when more were wasted, caught at Shiloh dancing. All that they had was the thread of togetherness. And the faint hope that, after the concubine from Bethlehem, someone would go up there and begin again.

My God, in anguish, dread, and speechless pain, I await a sign of gentleness. I welcome the untouched woman who brings forth a reverent man. Mother and Messiah I might name them.

QUESTIONS FOR REFLECTION AND DISCUSSION

• In Judges, there are sites associated with bloodshed and horror, like Mt. Tabor and Bethlehem, which become in the gospels places of miracle, gentleness, and grace. How does this kind of counterpoint of events strike you? What does it say to you about the meaning of "redemption"?

• The women in the Gibeah story are victimized and brutalized in a number of ways. In what ways does the shared experience of senseless tragedy prompt sisterhood and solidarity? Where do you see that today?

Ruth, the Disciple-in-Law

(Read Ruth 1–4)

Ruth said: "Do not press me to leave you and to stop going with you, for wherever you go, I shall go, wherever you live, I shall live. Your people will be my people, and your God will be my God." Ruth 1:16

AT LAST there was a more civilized story to tell over. Ruth must have been one of those women who sat out at night watching fields bronze under full moon. Her mother-in-law, her friend, was also a star-follower who caught the closest as well as the farthest glow. They were light in loss and in life. They were light in love. They must have noticed and wondered and dreamed and spoken their fantasies beyond dusk as dampness dallied down.

Ruth, Naomi, theirs was an earthly loyalty of sheaf by sheaf, birth by death, tugging loneliness by someone to stay with, wisdom by uncertainty, affiliation and family by pain, step by step. Ruth knew where to go and with whom. Naomi knew what to say. Virtue knew means of introduction. Availability knew how to husband—barley fields or harvesters or threshing floors or well-fed men. Boaz knew a good removed cousin and a captivating in-law when he found them.

While she went through David and ended with Jesus, Ruth began with Naomi, herself, and her son. That mother-in-law, wherever she went, was a woman of feeling and freedom, a woman of God, a winning woman who held the other in the simple mystery of her warmth and calm. They bonded blessedness before anyone was born.

I thank you, Lord, for the models and mothers who ease me along the way. For friendship and gentle persuasion, for faithfulness and new life, I am grateful. You have given me bonds of love, adoption, and family, and I find you surely and somehow in them.

QUESTIONS FOR REFLECTION AND DISCUSSION

• There is much talk of "mentoring" these days. In what ways does Naomi qualify as a mentor? What characteristics of a worthy mentor does she display?

• Ruth comes across as a loyal disciple and steadfast friend. What qualities of lasting feminine friendship do you find highlighted in the Ruth-Naomi story?

HANNAH AT PRAYER

(Read 1 Samuel 1-2)

Hannah replied, "I am a woman in great trouble; I have not been drinking wine or strong drink—I am pouring out my soul before Yahweh." 1 Samuel 1:15

ON THE ASH HEAP she had tears and the fine old flakes of everything that had burned down. She could not eat even simple bread nor sip water. By the Shiloh shrine she moved her lips with words only God could hear. The priest, puzzled up from his seat, prayed for anything. Hannah sat in the wind until, coming back to cheer and the grim possibility of try-try-again, she could take meals and Elkanah. She became like a tent billowing.

The son Samuel was the phoenix from her tired, squat, gray fire. He was promised to her as riches, success, and the wisdom of old wives' tales fell under the last smoke of her years of unfulfilled desire. When that new flame was fanned and her tent filled, there was food. Hannah had spoken her peace. The God of Eli had caught on like the last tentative piece of kindling. She could cook, feed, and finally eat as never till then.

Fill me, Lord, with life and Godsend. Give me readiness, slowly, to billow and burn. Grant me courage, Lord, to start something. When?

QUESTIONS FOR REFLECTION AND DISCUSSION

• Hannah's prayer might be described as "the prayer of abandonment" or even "the prayer of desperation." How is such prayer creative and renewing? When have you experienced it?

• Comment on the similarities, the parallels, between Hannah's song of praise (1 Samuel 2:1-10) and Mary's Magnificat (Luke 1:46–55). What do you consider the central message of these prayers?

MICHAL, DAVID'S FIRST

(Read 1 Samuel 18:20–30; 19:1–18; 25:42–44)

Jonathan, Saul's son, held David in great affection; and Jonathan warned David, "My father Saul is looking for a way to kill you...." Michal, David's wife, warned him, "If you do not escape tonight, you will be a dead man tomorrow!" 1 Samuel 19:2,11

SHE CAME and went, this wife of a moment who madly loved, saved his life, then was traded off in her father's miff.

In the end it was her brother Jonathan's love for his friend that prevailed and was readily memorialized in poem, song, dance, bronze, or stone.

There were different ties of love. The token of hers was a dummy-god in the bed topped with a mat of goat hair while her husband slid down the house and ran like hellfire over the hill rather than staying (round circles, round circles) to be a father-in-law's spear target. It was quick unknotting.

Jonathan's love was active and much. Michal's love was, for short time and serendipity, enough.

Lord, help me to settle with stepping into someone's life briefly, lending a hand, and stepping out again. I realize that you have many hands and use them to soothe, lift, and rescue as they come forward and go. Help me to remember that I do not need to stay longer than my short role requires. You are, after all, the one who tidies up, smooths over, makes good, and consoles.

QUESTIONS FOR REFLECTION AND DISCUSSION

• Michal's story is an odd one of love and loss. David paid a price for loving the king's daughter; she paid a price for loving an enviable warrior. How would you, or do you, deal with a hard-won love that costs dearly, lasts briefly, and then (for whatever reason) fritters off?

• Michal's story indicates that, while she rebelled against her father Saul, he also, in the end, controlled her, even to the point of "giving her" to a new husband. Share your understanding of patriarchy and explain how it was possible for a man to exercise such power over a daughter's fate.

ABIGAIL

(Read 1 Samuel 25)

David said to Abigail, "Blessed be Yahweh, God of Israel, who sent you to meet me today! Blessed be your wisdom and blessed you yourself for today having restrained me from the crime of bloodshed and from exacting revenge!" 1 Samuel 25:32–33

PERCEPTIVE, EMINENTLY PRACTICAL, a stunning beauty, and married to a fool, she came appeasing the angry, spurned warrior—with loaves, wine, sheep, grain, raisins, fig cakes, weighed-down donkeys, all in procession before her. She was suave, apologetic, obeisant, predictive. And David's wild nerves, taut muscles, set jaw, stiff neck let loose. He greeted peace and watched her walk.

Conveniently her husband died. She spent the rest of her life appeasing the new one, David, reminding him: The man of God, the anointed king, ought not be so brutal, so clumsily bloodthirsty, that he awakens with his rage spent but his soul lost the next morning.

Lord, let me bear gifts, play fair, and tame the power of your strong until mercy becomes the everyday ending, the favored bent of everyone.

QUESTIONS FOR REFLECTION AND DISCUSSION

• Among many other things, Abigail was the calmer of David's resentment and rage. How do you see women today exerting a gentling influence on society? How better can women be the voice of sense and reason in a warring world?

• Abigail's first encounter with David was political. In what sort of situations—political or otherwise—do you feel called to do some intervention, to make direct efforts to change the course of things?

THE LOVER BATHSHEBA

(Read 2 Samuel 11:1-12:24)

It happened towards evening when David had got up from resting and was strolling on the palace roof, that from the roof he saw a woman bathing; the woman was very beautiful....David then sent messengers to fetch her. She came to him.... . 2 Samuel 11:2,4

FEW PEOPLE KNEW what she was like or what she wanted except that she was enchanting and that she went along.

The affair began with a languorous rooftop view and ended, more or less, in the presto marriage of the widow.

She was complicit and compliant.

When Nathan admonished David, she admitted too that impulse had given way to impassioned action had given way to pregnant effect had given way to perplexity had given way to death had given way to regret. What was next but starting over with the upstart? David paid his bedtimes in worry and glum fast and a lovechild's death. Bathsheba paid in ache and long labor and an infant cold as stone. David woke up the next day, dressed up, and ate sumptuously.

Few people knew what she was like or what she wanted except that she decided to throw her arms around him and hold him as if she were meeting for the first time someone she had dreamed of. In reality she had stood in shadow and had lost and wept. She was complicit and compliant. After sin and sorrow she knew there was nothing to do but sunshine, hello my love, smile.

The next time she had a son named Solomon. David remembered God. She went along.

God of the ever-beginning, redeem my mistakes and sins until I am again both lover and laugher. Let me remember you in impulse, act, affection, and every going along.

QUESTIONS FOR REFLECTION AND DISCUSSION

• Through the ages, the attention of students of Scripture has been drawn to David's sin, his chastisement by Nathan, and his repentance. But what of Bathsheba? What would you consider her role and responsibility—or that of any consenting adult—in adultery? What factors might have limited her freedom of choice?

• Solomon's character might be described as splendid, wise, prodigal, and wild. What would you surmise might have been the influence of his parents on his character-formation? What good qualities and what lapses might you ascribe to his "taking after" mother and/or father?

TAMAR, DAVID'S DAUGHTER

(Read 2 Samuel 13)

Tamar put dust on her head, tore the magnificent dress which she was wearing, laid her hand on her head, and went away, crying aloud as she went. 2 Samuel 13:19

SHE WAS ULTIMATE among the lost and innocent. The offense, staggering: the rough lust of a half-brother, jewels stolen from a future husband, the pure gift ruptured and hammer-smashed in his own palace, the king's. And she unspeakably bruised and hurting.

Amnon's debt of death seemed fitting. Absalom's just sword understood wielding. But no one says the rest. What died in Tamar? Did she ever cease crying wildly, and for how long? Or could she never speak, never step into a room without flinching again? What dreams and night sweats beset her? What dread of serving meals? What apprehension of seemingly ill persons? Was there anyone who could be with her? Did her mind babble off, and did she want to be young again? Or would she go infantile? Go farther still, enwombed? Could she trust, at least, God? And, if she ever listened, could she feel God's lullaby, a healing hand, a restful charm?

David, meanwhile, daily mourned his son.

O wild, wild Lord, protect the son, the daughter. Prevent the quake, the rape. We cannot seem to keep ourselves. Without you, weak, dismayed, we break. Hold our torn hearts. And keep us from the worse-yet breaks we make.

QUESTIONS FOR REFLECTION AND DISCUSSION

• We might well wonder whether this Tamar, like any victim of incest or sexual abuse, ever regained the capacity for trust.

What do you see as the predictable struggles and the hopeful possibilities for someone in her situation to recover trust in family? in God?

• Share your understanding of the roles played by friendship, psychotherapy, and spiritual direction in the recovery of a victim of incest/abuse.

The Harlots of Squabble, Life, and Death

(Read 1 Kings 3:4-28)

The woman who was the mother of the living child addressed the king, for she felt acutely for her son. "I beg you, my Lord," she said, "let them give her the live child; on no account let them kill him!" But the other said, "He shall belong to neither of us. Cut him in half!" 1 Kings 3:26

WHEN HE WAS ANOINTED king, the pied, piped people nearly split the earth with their hurrahing. When he had sat awhile, the woman came, hysteric and huffy, who would have split a baby, and another.

Solomon had his wives, seven hundred of them, and three hundred or so incidental other women. In between the confusion of their gods and his labor camps, he practiced wisdom. When he practiced, it was wonderful, sheer gift of intelligence, grasp, integrity, soul-seeing. Solomon discerned beyond the borders of himself and thus found the right woman for the case.

No matter how many of his own women had been mistaken, and had mistaken him, there was this one sure mother, the one who would save life. The one who would let breath and soft flesh and baby gurgling be, no matter whether she ever again held, nursed, cradled, burped, or rocked to sleep.

He knew a mother, he whose own had waked a near-dead king to prophet, hornblow, priestly oil, and the processional on mule. Like Bathsheba, this one woman, in the dispute of the baby, poured cries of "Long live! Long live!" about the king.

Solomon heard.

She rang true.

To life, O God, to life, no matter what the price. Let me be heartened— and mother, however bereft, of those who survive.

Questions for Reflection and Discussion

• The case of the two harlots seems clearly to be a dispute between a woman who prized possession and a woman who prized life. How, in your own life, do you sometimes treat possession as a priority? How does society in general show, at times, that possession is a priority? How can you personally be truer to the choice for life? What would it take to convert society in general to a more pervasive choice for life?

THE QUEEN OF SHEBA

(Read 1 Kings 10:1–26; 11:1–13)

The queen of Sheba heard of Solomon's fame and came to test him with difficult questions....Not one of them was too obscure for the king to answer for her. 1 Kings 10:1,3

JOURNEYING TOWARD LEGEND, curious, quizzical, she came. The man, his wit, his breadth of knowing, his understanding heart, his charm, his opulence, the cheer and majesty of his house and all surrounding him dazzled the brown queen. Her camels waddled with the weight of more and more, a tonnage of goods for one who had and seemed to be the receiver of everything.

In amazement, awe, the insecurity of bright surprise, she asked: What riverhead? What wellspring? What irrepressible stream spilled down the mountain, gushing and gathering, pouring into this fresh ocean of rich gift?

That which swam and danced and spoke beyond her ken alluded to a source elsewhere—to a grand Intelligence, a comprehender of cosmos and elastic tidbits, a benevolent proprietor, philanthropist, safekeeper. Solomon was, for her, a sample of a farther Someone whose whereabouts she asked, whom she now hoped to meet.

Solomon knew. She would have expected his abundant, lavish God to have been, ever and endlessly, enough for him. The God whose rivulets she now could track seemed so, so certainly enough for her.

I want, God the length, God the height, God the depth of everything, to see more truly, to grasp, to accept with grateful heart your everlasting gifts. Let me be satiate and glad, awake and faithful to your flowing wisdom.

QUESTIONS FOR REFLECTION AND DISCUSSION

• The African woman traveled exceeding distance and brought much of her wealth as an offering to attain the one thing she was wanting: wisdom. Where and to whom would you, do you, go? What would you be willing to sacrifice, let go of, lay at someone else's service to gain wisdom yourself?

THE WIDOW OF ZAREPHATH

(Read 1 Kings 17)

The woman went and did as Elijah told her. 1 Kings 17:15

SHE HAD THE BARE BONES of almost nothing. And she was almost alone, but for her son. They were almost ready to starve, to sink down listless into death. She gave the foreign man a bite, a sip, as she collected almost her last sticks.

It was almost miracle. She kept baking flour cakes from the almost empty jar and almost zeroed jug of oil.

Elijah ate. She, too. And the son.

She gave him shelter under a roof almost blown apart, brittle, holed, dried out in drought-wind. She let the prophet sleep on a straw bed almost eaten by animals. It was all.

Her scrawny son was sick and dead. Elijah breathed. His great, rich-winded God gave back a life. The hollow widow had nothing left to feel but almost surprise.

There is almost an end, a time when I find nothing left but a famine of feeling and sense. When I am almost in that void, Lord, let me still invite another in and give.

QUESTIONS FOR REFLECTION AND DISCUSSION

• Pope John Paul II has exhorted Americans to "give of your substance, not just your abundance" (Yankee Stadium, 1979). How would life and the world in general be different if we truly did that?

• What do you suppose would give someone like the widow in this story both the motivation and the strength to take a chance on exhausting all her resources to respond to someone else's need? Could you?

AZUBAH

(Read 1 Kings 22:41–51 and 2 Chronicles 20:5–34)

Jehoshaphat bowed his head, his face to the ground, and all Judah and the citizens of Jerusalem fell down before Yahweh to worship....His mother's name was Azubah daughter of Shilhi. 2 Chronicles 20:18,31

WE DO NOT KNOW whether she was gray-haired, a trifle whis-kered, plump, bent at the knees when she was old.

This is all we recollect: that she was reverent and respectful. That she had a good and prayerful son. That her great-great-great-great-ad infinitum-grandson was in the line of Jehoshaphat and called the Christ.

God, give me grace to know that it is all right to be part of some long line. Let me be content, though I do not know quite where I go.

Questions for Reflection and Discussion

• Recall some of your own "venerable ancestors" in faith, in family, in the encouragement of your own fulfillment and freedom. Who were they, and why have they been so important in your becoming who you are?

ANOTHER WIDOW WITH OIL,
AND A WOMAN OF INFLUENCE
(Read 2 Kings 4)

Elisha said [to the widow], "What can I do for you?" [And to the Shunammite woman he said,] "Look, you have gone to all this trouble for us, what can we do for you?" 2 Kings 4:2,13

THE MAN OF GOD had a gift for multiplication—jars of oil, barley bread, edible stew, the days of children's lives.

The widow of the guild prophet received enough jugged oil to sell and saved her dears from slavery. The Shunammite received the unasked, unexpected son and, later, his revival from the crazed, chill bed of death.

Both women had reverence; both, generosity; both, faith—each in her way. They lived through desperation into gladder endings.

Elisha said their miracles were the wages of knowing whom to ask and when to hold whose feet.

Lord, let me recognize the ones who stand for you. Let me readily seek help from those who spend your Spirit. I need not only to give freely but to learn how freely to receive.

QUESTIONS FOR REFLECTION AND DISCUSSION

• What unexpected "rewards" and benefits have you received when you have been humble enough to ask someone for help?

• Recount your personal history with the prayer of petition. When have you been "answered" by God specifically and directly? When has your answer seemed to be a non-answer? How often, and for what, do you petition God these days?

NAAMAN'S SLAVE
(Read 2 Kings 5)

"This and this," he reported, "is what the girl from Israel has said." 2
Kings 5:4

THE SMALL GIRL said to the woman of her scabrous, ill, and
white commander, "Go to Samaria, and find the prophet there."
   Later she thought: He has a clue of living water. And certainly:
Do whatever he tells you.
   Naaman neither turned to wine nor ran to tell the townspeople.
He balked. But afterwards he hauled back Israeli soil and praised
the God of healing powers.
   The slavechild shut her eyes awhile and smiled.

*God, grant me confidence in you, your power, and your will to make all
well—even the ones who are silly about it, even the ones who borrow advice and then argue.*

QUESTIONS FOR REFLECTION AND DISCUSSION

• The slave girl made a referral. How well do you do with rec-
ommending other, more qualified sources of help when people
come to you? That is, how well do you recognize situations which
call not only for a listening ear but for expertise?
   • Can you accept simple, direct suggestions for your own
physical, emotional, mental, or spiritual well-being and at least
give them a try? Or do you immediately write off suggestions as
too trivial, insufficient, or a waste of time? Why, either way?

THE DESPOT ATHALIAH

(Read 2 Kings 8:26; 11:1–20; 2 Chronicles 22,23)

When Athaliah mother of Ahaziah learned that her son was dead, she promptly murdered all those of royal stock. 2 Kings 11:1

DAVID HAD BEEN PROMISED an eternal lamp. The people had been asked to keep the wick of fidelity trimmed.

Now and again there would be, among them, a blood-mother, a tyrant who usurped the holy line even as she belonged to it, seized and slew and made idolatry simple.

Perhaps she went crackpot after her son fell. Perhaps an insanity of corpse upon corpse numbed what little love might have felt its way through her. Perhaps her soul froze in the storm of power after power after power.

She was no better than the worst of David's sons. She readied the people for her opposite—in their own defense and with relief sighs, chasms wide. Thus, they were grateful for her scarcely saved grandson, for his goodness and devotion.

In spite of herself, the grim grandmother begot Joash, a godly king. She had just missed him in the dark.

The lamplighter made another round.

O God, make good. Turn evil days of formless mass to sturdy shape with a human face to your own likeness; turn black patch over the reckless, gouged-out eye of night; turn the sighted-eye shot with fury, blood, and harm; turn the gone and blind, the seer and the lookout in haze alike: to daybreak calm and light; turn vengeful parent to guileless child and reconcile. Trim us, God. Begin us again.

QUESTIONS FOR REFLECTION AND DISCUSSION

• Revenge, bloodthirstiness, and contempt all seem sadly within the realm of human possibility. When you attempt to understand, do you find that you can grasp at least a bit of what must be the workings of a poisoned mind and a hardened heart? How do you explain murderers? tyrants?

• Are you sufficiently in touch with the dark side of yourself to acknowledge the potential for evil there? If so, how do you explain the fact that you do not activate that potential?

HEPHZIBAH
(Read 2 Kings 21:1–18 and 2 Chronicles 33:1–20)

While in his distress, he placated Yahweh his God by genuinely humbling himself before the God of his ancestors. When Mannasseh prayed...[God] was moved by his entreaty, heard his supplication and brought him back to Jerusalem to his kingdom. Manasseh realized then that Yahweh is God. 2 Chronicles 33:12–13

MANASSEH, FATHER OF AMON, who was father of Josiah, who was father of Jechoniah before the exile, whose descendant was Joseph the husband of Mary, was Hephzibah's son. Her husband Hezekiah received Isaiah and all his prophecies and signs.

The shadow would fall back ten steps. The virgin would give birth.

Enough. Except.

Manasseh turned sick, wild, worshipped sticks and stone idols, burned his son alive, summoned ghosts, smiled in the bloodbath. So the writing says.

What is not written are the tears of his mother: for the madness, for the years of milk and nurturance gone to mess, for dismay and loss, for the shadow that falls when it should be high noon.

What is not written are the pleas of Hephzibah, nor her surprise at the moment when Manasseh turned, in chains, and adored the abandoned God of Israel. Time and again she had raised her kingchild up. Suddenly and unawares, she, in a scowl of prayer, gave birth to memory, to pious, ancient, now reclaimed forebears.

Good God, I pray with the staying faith of those in graves who saw and taught us better ways. For years and years, with thankful praise, I await the change of heartbeats, of silent tears, of days.

QUESTIONS FOR REFLECTION AND DISCUSSION

• Speak a bit about the pain of a parent whose child has "gone wrong," whose offspring has deserted the beliefs and values of his or her upbringing. What recourse is there for mothers and fathers in such a predicament?

HULDAH THE PROPHETESS
(Read 2 Kings 22)

The priests Hilkiah, Ahikam, Achbor, Shaphan and Asaiah went to the prophetess Huldah wife of Shallum son of Tikvah, son of Harhas the keeper of the wardrobe; she lived in Jerusalem in the new town. 2 Kings 22:14

IN THOSE DAYS they sent smoke to Baal and to everything in the wide sky. When Hilkiah found and Shaphan read the book of the Law and told the king, Josiah wept and ripped the heart of everything. A cleansing began.

Huldah called them back. With pledges and threats of what would come (though his eyes would not see), she cheered Josiah on to redoing, redoing worship, allegiance, fidelity, priests, altars, pillars, sacrifice, tombs, suppers, spirits, and the uses of women. She was as certain and strong as consonants cut clear and deep in stone.

Huldah, all unlettered, had waited and waited some more for the unread law. Somehow, meanwhile, she had been knowing, seeing, memorizing its pictures as they had been drawn in her heart: "Hear, O Israel...."

The woman Huldah was the appropriate mouthpiece and spokesperson, thoughtful in silence, careful of tongue, attended to, uttering God's good, entering into her place and day, seizing divine time, and departing gracefully when her moment passed.

Lord of all ages, may I, may we, intuit your law, even before we find it all. May we feel your pulse, read you, turn every which way, redound, go glory, and rest, O lovely, in being what we see.

QUESTIONS FOR REFLECTION AND DISCUSSION

• Huldah was an intuitive, one who could read clearly the law of God within her heart. How can such intuition be developed and found trustworthy? How does one become "pure of heart"?

The Weeping Women

(Read Psalm 137, Ezra, and Nehemiah)

"We survive only as the remnant we are today. We come before you in our guilt; because of it we cannot stand in your presence." While Ezra was praying and making confession, a very large crowd of men, women and children of Israel gathered round him, the people weeping bitterly. Ezra 9:15–10:1

AFTER THE WHIRLPOOLS of Babylon, after harps hung in underbrush and high trees, after remembering, the women stood dazed, tentative, and shed soft tears.

Cyrus had sent them home to all of Israel. Cyrus had given provisions to rebuild the temple in Jerusalem. They dwelt again, tending, resting in their own. The Lord dwelt with them, honored, known. They shed soft tears for sin, grace, exile, comeback. Quietly, they cried for all their history.

They wept when the building began, when suspicion halted it, and when Darius decreed the building should resume. They wept when Ezra spoke and prayed, when Ezra sat sadly still in his torn clothes. They wept for foreigners, their sisters, who were to be separated and sent. They wept for the new fences, the old tribes, the new lives, the old requirements. They wept for purgation and purity. With the men and children, they wept while Ezra read the Moses scroll. They wept till Nehemiah ordered: Party! Eat! Smile with the God who smiles in hardship! Smile, o my people, in your strength and your worn souls!

Could it have been, could it have been, that all these decades the arms of God had been loosely keeping them? Could it have been all through Babylon? They tried to blot their eyes and smile at what still could be.

With these people, O God of harsh expectations yet God of ease and mercy, I give in. My amen is to my need, your irresistible will. My amen is

to my survival, your conditions. God, I would, and I sometimes want to,
bend to your blessings, by the book.

QUESTIONS FOR REFLECTION AND DISCUSSION

• The right to renew the Covenant and to restore the full obser-
vance of the law was cause for celebration but also for heartache.
Relate the experience of the women who had returned from Babylon to an experience of your own when you were caught in a cycle
of hope, setback, and hope again.

Anna in Nineveh, Edna and Sarah of Media

(Read Tobit)

Without more ado, Raguel committed Sarah his bride into his keeping. He gave Tobiah half his wealth, slaves, men and women, oxen and sheep, donkeys and camels, clothes and money and household things. And so he let them leave happily....To his daughter Sarah he said, "Go now to your father-in-law's house, since henceforward they are as much your parents as those who gave you life." Tobit 10:10, 12

WAN SARAH, of the unlucky smothered husbands, did not know that a blind old man a long walk away was praying for death while she was begging of God her own escape.

Anna, the weaver of cloth who bickered with her old goat over the young goat she was paid, did not know that her long-gone only son was reveling his wedding nights away under an angel's fine blessing rather than slumping twisted in a ditch waiting for a kaddish.

Edna, after she baked bread and made up the newlyweds' bedroom, did not know whether or not her maid would find that her new son-in-law had died of her innocent, cursed daughter.

They did, however, know that their men prayed their confidence, surprise, and praise. They did know that Tobit and Raguel dug burial holes and that Tobiah's God could smoke out demons.

They found out later that everyone lived happily and in safety and that seven sons, an infinity, more than made up for seven near-miss husbands and the onlyness of two children.

They lived on, after Raphael owned up, knowing that there were healing angels and companions carrying them back and forth, to and from God's throne.

God of good spirits and the knowledge of everything, send me the angel of confidence to wait for your glad-made finale.

Questions for Reflection and Discussion

• Elements of magic and superstition mingle in the Tobit story with faith and religion. Where in the story do you find examples of the deepest faith?

• "Angels Watching Over Me" has long been a theme for Christian song and story. How would you explain to a nonbeliever the notion of angels? Have you ever had a personal sense of an angel or angels in your own life?

JUDITH, THE STARTLING ONE
AMONG GORGEOUS MOURNERS

(Read Judith, especially 8–16)

When they saw Judith, her face so changed and her clothes so different,
they were lost in admiration of her beauty. They said to her:
  May the God of our ancestors keep you in his favor!
  May he crown your designs with success
  to the glory of the children of Israel,
  to the greater glory of Jerusalem! Judith 10:7–8

THE WAG MIGHT SAY she dressed to kill.

The truer teller of the story would remember her drab mourning wraps and her squats on the roof. The gold, the gems, the finery, the sensuous rich flush of cloth appeared when she feared she might live to see not only her husband's but her whole race's demise. She had to do something against the oppressor. It would be some sort of diversion, and she was surer than she was sure of her near-knit maid that the Almighty would turn the trick and give gumption for whatever.

Judith was a subtle, wise, devout woman, the kind whom doubters consulted, the shunned fled to for welcome, the grieving turned to for calm. In everything Judith listened. Most of the time she barely moved. She heard, they spoke, the world shifted, and there was a God again. But once a span of decades had ground on and the defeatists were twirling purposes and walking backwards into their plan, she became a siren.

She was a single-minded sacred opportunist. The gentle woman raged at the nearness of betrayal, at the sell-out of a people. She had no tender scruples about Holofernes. For her, the sword thwacking his neck was no murder weapon; instead, it was the agent of an act of God, of the rescue of the chosen, of the smashing of an idol. Holofernes' tyrannical body seemed no temple to her, but rather a blasphemous throne where a thousand devils saluted and brandished their armor and blades.

After the death of the drunken destroyer, the people sang; they hailed her. She again was quiet and empty. She put on her old robes and her most unspectacular face.

To Judith, slaying an enemy in God's name, with God's might, was little more than finding enough water and baking flat cakes for the day. It was for family. It kept them alive. They drank. They ate.

I pray the prayer of Judith, Lord, as uncanny as it may be and as hard to grasp: Strength of the numberless, power of the nobodies, aid for the helpless, handstand for those without arms, hear my prayer now, please, for you are Creator, Remaker; you are Doer of all great deeds.

QUESTIONS FOR REFLECTION AND DISCUSSION

• The widow Judith is a type of contemplative moved to dramatic action. How do you see the call to both contemplation and action played out in your own life? What do you consider to be characteristic of a contemplative vocation?

• Once again we see a Jewish heroine engaged in a violent action. This raises the persistent question: Under what circumstances, under what threat to a nation or people, do you feel violence might be justified?

ESTHER, THE BRAZEN QUEEN

(Read Esther)

Esther sent this reply to Mordecai, "Go and assemble all the Jews now in Susa and fast for me. Do not eat or drink day or night for three days. For my part, I and my waiting-women shall keep the same fast, after which I shall go to the king in spite of the law; and if I perish, I perish." Esther 4:15–16

ONCE UPON A TIME there was a dazzling queen. She delivered her people from the lion's mouth and a dragon dream. She did it by prayer and fainting.

King Ahaseurus was mighty and flip-flop. Though his consort, she hardly liked him. As she told her God, the queenship made sense only if it had a bizarre purpose. She would just as leave not. She took her chances and upset decorum. She went to his majesty, praying and fainting. Then she called a banquet. She bargained that marked lives could be handed back and that death warrants and the law of cast lots could be hastily remanded. Ahaseurus admired her originality. Or maybe her looks. He gave her anything in a reminder and fine wines.

Esther won by prayer and fainting. Her people released their enemies. They celebrated Purim by her uncle's decree. He, luckily, was second to the king. She hardly knew her people but ordered yes, too: make festivity.

Mordecai overheard things and kept his old nightmares in mind. They had a bizarre purpose. Esther reigned by prayer and fainting.

I, too, can be alone in an unhappy spot. Let my place do good for someone, God. You save your people. Some of mine are away, bygone, estranged, and I cannot.

QUESTIONS FOR REFLECTION AND DISCUSSION

• Esther did not truly choose her "vocation," her location, or her occupation in the court of Ahaseurus (Xerxes). Can you recount a story from your own life or from hearsay in which a person who was unhappily placed in life was able to accomplish something terribly important by having been "in the right place at the right time"?

• Learn what you can about Purim and share what you have found about the meaning of the feast.

THE TOUGH MOTHER OF THE MACCABEES

(Read 2 Maccabees 7)

The mother was especially admirable and worthy of honorable remembrance, for she watched the death of seven sons in the course of a single day, and bravely endured it because of her hopes in the Lord. 2 Maccabbes 7:20

THERE WAS SOME POINT at which the believer who really believed and lived on that belief was finally zeroed in on. She knew that. It came down to dire choice.

Life turned and woke from one day to the next on that little limit, this twist, that change of plans or mind, this smidgen of a compromise. But the step which would modify or waive or ease or exempt the deeper symbols of religion, the deeper faithfulness, was the step she would not take. There was an empty no in her voice, in her laboring chest, in the center of her bones, and in her memories of childbirth.

To eat was fine. To make a sham of the law, an expedient pretense, was, Eleazar before had known, to make a joke of God and every good from Moses down.

She told her last son. He agreed that his zero hour had come. The line had been drawn, and he would not step across it.

For her it was dark irony. To hold his life, by one quick concession, one small so-what, would be the simplest. All that was needed was a gesture, a fib. She would rather that her last son die. It would be another honest death. Even if for an untaken bite of pig meat. He would be the hungry man saying, "I will not swallow your gods; I will not eat a lie."

She had an intuition that the unfed son, the last cruel death, would wait for her with the others somewhere. She felt that there would be more to their story.

My God, help me to discern the symbols, the messages, in my actions.

Guide my judgment so that I may know the essential from the dispensable, the vital from the trivial. And so let me hold to the true for dear life. Or death.

QUESTIONS FOR REFLECTION AND DISCUSSION

• The mother of the Maccabees was uncompromising. What would you consider a cause significant enough that it would be worth the life of someone dear to you or worth your own dying?

• How does the Christmas-tide celebration of Hanukkah relate to the story of the Maccabees?

JOB'S OTHERS
(Read Job 1:13–21; 38:1–42:6; 42:13–17)

Throughout the land there were no women as beautiful as the daughters of Job. And their father gave them inheritance rights like their brothers. After this, Job lived for another one hundred and forty years, and saw his children and his children's children to the fourth generation. Job 42:15–16

HE CAME FROM a naked mother.

His wife berated his innocence and recommended: Give up. Give in. Curse God. Drop dead.

His first three daughters and seven sons crushed and smothered in their wine supper when the house fell in.

Day after day he asked, complained, answered, mused till he had plumbed the secrets of the universe and knew that he had not been there and couldn't understand.

He taught these mysteries to Jemimah, to Keziah, to Keren-happuch, the daughters of his restoration.

They grew up at peace with ruin and prosperity and held loosely to their children and their charms. They inherited what Job had to give them from his hard learning. Theirs was the spirit of anything.

The dove flew to God.

The perfume scented the halls of heaven.

The powder shadowing the eyes showed as they closed calmly and sifted the secrets of the divine.

They were true to their names.

The three comprehended that they did not comprehend. They remembered that they had not been there when the wide world was a-making. They were sure that they couldn't recall a thing before their birthing. They knew, however, who was, who did: the voice that Dad heard, in the thunder.

You are too great, O God, too many in dimension. Remind me that I am the philosopher who knows best that she does not know much about anything. Help me to know those things in you, in sounds and glimmerings, in reverbs and whatevering.

QUESTIONS FOR REFLECTION AND DISCUSSION

• The names of Job's few daughters had special meaning, even on a spiritual level: Jemimah (dove), Keziah (perfume), Keren-Happuch (eyeshadow). What names of people close to you have been chosen because of a special meaning or association?

• The end to Job's suffering carried evident "restitution" for his endurance, his faithfulness, and his submission. Aside from the exterior rewards, what interior rewards (consolations, transformations, reconciliation) did Job win from his encounters with tragedy and loss?

THE WOMAN OF PRAYER:
THE SOUL OF PSALMS
(Read Psalm 141:1–2)

May my prayer be like incense in your presence, my uplifted hands like the evening sacrifice. Psalm 141:2

SHE LEANED HER HEAD against the chill, damp wall near the faint flap of the window covers. She turned her head, right, and with her left arm, her left hand, her, for now, vague fingers, she flipped the drape an inch or two away from wall and window. She looked in a lasting laze into the night lake, into the far island of evening star and sure, phantasmagoric shapes, dot by dot. She whispered of the starlight: praise.

She had been alone for a long, long time, and she felt barely form or strength to beckon, to hail, to touch, to clasp back whatever offered hand came through her air. The lake above her and the lights therein drew closer. She began again, aloud. The steam of her words puffed up and out and dissipated across cold miles. Just then she felt Someone. She felt the arms that caught her askings and her baffled admiration and cupped them. She felt Someone. She felt the waiting one who raised her worded breath to a left ear, like shell alive with echo, and listened as to ocean. A night breeze ticked.

She was all alone, and there were two of them.

She made a cloud of Amen.

God of no space, God of never time, break in, so that this lonely once I may know you are. Touch me, God, O gently, now.

QUESTIONS FOR REFLECTION AND DISCUSSION

• When your prayer rises "like incense" to the Lord, what do you send up in that smoke? How much of your prayer is typically adoration and praise? How much is contrition or regret? How much is thanksgiving? How much is request?

• How does prayer affect your ability to deal with loneliness? How do you distinguish aloneness from loneliness?

THE GOOD WIFE
(Read Proverbs 31:10–31)

Her children stand up and proclaim her blessed, her husband, too, sings her praises: "Many women have done admirable things, but you surpass them all!" Proverbs 31:28–29

SHE WAS CANNY and clear, savvy and sure. From youth she laid claim to her birthright, knew her gifts, honed her skills, and foresaw endless possibilities. She was a steward of goods who was graceful with strangers' and servants' and children's souls.

For her, it was a matter of reverence. It was a matter of gratitude. The pearl, her allurement, was the pure, hidden pulse of being. She extended her arms and was swept in the spiral, like a lithe danceuse under a spell—the spiral of yesterdays and todays that wind into tomorrow.

A midwife of providence, she was mother, too, of the confident now.

Creator God, let me be with the being of creation and glide giving, into the future. Make me a wise woman, a lasting likeness of you.

QUESTIONS FOR REFLECTION AND DISCUSSION

• Numerous lists have been made of the "natural" qualities and gifts of femininity. What do you consider the "natural" gifts of women in relation to the earth itself and the earth's children?

THE BELOVED OF SONGS

(Read the Song of Songs)

Come then, my beloved, my lovely one, come.
For see the winter is past, the rains are over and gone.
Flowers are appearing on the earth.
The season of glad songs has come. Song of Songs 2:10–12

SHE WAS THE BODY language of the soul.

When the lily-browser missed her among the sheep, the woman loped and lunged around the town like a crazy. Yet his gaze was worshipful. He pictured her in the clothes of birth, in a wedding dress, in jewels.

She pictured him as the earth itself, the strongest tree, a buck, a gazelle, a king.

They sought and courted across nut gardens and hills, across fluffs of sheep and lily stalks, across apples and dry grapes, across doves. They called each other's names till they bounced off cavern walls and temple ceilings.

After a frivolous hide-and-seek, they found. They embraced.

The sheep, the hills, the gardens, the doves, the lilies, the skies, the apple trees, the grapevines, and every sane watcher on the streets fell lost. The lookouts faced every which way. The earth went swirling. She was lost again and gladly descending, arising, rocking, swaying into deeper, more luscious, consuming loss. Where she was found, found, found.

Lovely.

Beloved.

At one.

In love.

Love, you are the end of my heart's longing—though I hardly know how to find and hold you, though I sometimes fear you are unreachably far off. Lead me, lure me, by long clues until I rest upon you and believe. I love, oh, what you are...and you. What I still need is to feel you here, ever-Real, and then to stay and stay until you so, so overtake me.

QUESTIONS FOR REFLECTION AND DISCUSSION

• Great contemplatives and mystics have often used the language of romance and erotic love to express their own pursuit and "falling in love" with God. What do you see as "romantic" in the best sense about the spiritual life? What role does passion play in the search for and experience of the Holy?

WOMANSPIRIT: WISDOM
(Read Genesis 1:1–2 and Wisdom 7:21–8:1)

She is a breath of the power of God, pure emanation of the glory of the Almighty. Wisdom 7:25

THE SPIRIT HOVERING over waters and within has always been. She is, and she always will be.

Wisdom is the Mediterranean that we swim in, the sea of every birth that gives.

Listen.

Wisdom, be attentive! Let me pray, O holy One, like a good Byzantine, with open ears, open eyes, open heart, open mind.

QUESTIONS FOR REFLECTION AND DISCUSSION

• A repeated call in the Byzantine liturgy is the one introducing this chapter's short prayer, "Wisdom, be attentive!" In the life of Solomon, the wisdom he requested is defined as "an understanding heart." When you ask for wisdom, what is it that you are asking for? When you feel you have been given wisdom, how do you experience it?

• Wisdom is named as a spiritual gift and an attribute of God, but wisdom is also at times identified with the Holy Spirit. To what extent can you say not only that God is Love but also that God is Wisdom? Explain.

THE BEST FRIEND
(Read Sirach 6:5–17)

A loyal friend is a powerful defense: whoever finds one has indeed found a treasure....A loyal friend is the elixir of life and those who fear the Lord will find one. Sirach 6:14,16

SHE WAS MORE than one who lived in the next house and recognized who was coughing at night, more than one who had met and chatted with and sometimes served spouse, children, far cousins, madcap uncles and aunts, stiff in-laws, and could chuckle and shrug about them too, more than one who walked along in pleasant talk with each day's water bucket or market satchel. She was more than one who remembered a special history of cares and questions and hopes and happy surprises shared. She was more even than one who stayed and stayed, and much more than her everlasting kindness.

She was one who often did not have to speak. She had the gift of long standby through delight or grief. She had an embrace that took in more than a dear one; a hand on the shoulder that made right a dizziness, a screaming fit, a grave mistake, a quizzical, desperate sin. She sensed, too, when to break silence and what to say when.

More yet, she was one who could tell roughly how many cups of God went into a breadloaf, what whisper of God stirred the waters, where God stood in a tent pole or hid in the house bricks. And she had long ago guessed that God was somewhat in a treasure chest and shining, though invisible; while more of God—and she sensed almost where—caught the shadow at noon and held it up against whatever tried to cast it, then a little later let it go and wiggled it around, then later still, at dark's pitch, filtered the starlight through the changing shapes of moon. She nearly knew.

God, great thanks for the sisters of my heart, the soul companions of my wanderings, for the one or maybe two who are more than themselves, more than steady friends, indeed great loves and sweeping panoramas of you.

QUESTIONS FOR REFLECTION AND DISCUSSION

• Sirach (Ecclesiasticus) offers its treatise on friendship, as have Cicero, Aelred of Rievaulx, Emerson, Lillian Hellman, and so many others in their writings. What is Christian friendship and how is it developed, tested, and made lasting?

• What can true friends reasonably expect and ask of one another?

THE VIRGIN AND THE VINEYARD
(Read Isaiah 5:1–7; 7:10–14)

Now, the vineyard of Yahweh Sabaoth is the House of Israel, and the
people of Judah the plant he cherished.... The young woman...will give
birth to a son whom she will call Immanuel. Isaiah 5:7; 7:14

WHILE THE MIND MAY well know and the body may brilliantly
express, there can be heartgap.

What Moses taught and Isaiah recalled in parables of vines and
wild grapes, a people still did not take in. Except for the rare ones,
whose names are on Godbooks or are buried with their bones.

Mostly they awaited dramatization. They readied, among
themselves, a woman to be. She would repair the breach, span the
gap, she would set Immanuel in the middle of things.

They hoped that they would remember then.

God-with-us, God-with-us, God-with-us. It rose like an acceler-
ating chant. The mind knew. The bodies went back to the vineyard work. One heart took shape slowly, cell by cell, in the heart
of God.

Much later, bands of women at prayer, circles of worshipping
men, would sing to her as root, her son as vine; to her as grape,
her son as wine. Her heart kept growing them.

O God, out of you sprang Mary, your Miriam.
Out of Miriam, you.
Out of you, us. You who are God within....

QUESTIONS FOR REFLECTION AND DISCUSSION

• How were the people of Yahweh (the vineyard) prepared for
the coming of the Messiah?

• What connections do you see between the Virgin Mary and
some (many?) of the foremothers of the Old Testament?

DAUGHTER ZION

(Read Lamentations)

Who can rescue and comfort you, young daughter of Zion? For huge as the sea is your ruin: who can heal you? Lamentations 2:13

SHE FELT THE FEEL of someone slinking in the house who shouldn't be there, the feel of shadow and clutched tool, the feel of tiptoe and taut throat, the fear of robbers prying loose the graves of gods, and awful answering in someone's outloud dream.

Outside, the night was fog, the glowing ice of cats' eyes out of Egypt, the sizzling snakes of Eden sidling under and into buildings, the stench of dead dogs, the hoot of brawlers, the desperate questions of scarred, thin women wafting through lewd streets.

She felt the cough of carrion, sad promises, dream visions fallen through amnesia traps. She wondered what, if any, good remained, what being waited where, what features were on what face.

Unless they were to be all lost, some light—indiscriminate, and of itself—must come.

Bright saving one, come rescue, come redeem. Secure your own, and beam into our sleep.

QUESTIONS FOR REFLECTION AND DISCUSSION

• Daughter Zion is at times identified with all of Israel and sometimes with the holy city, Jerusalem. Jesus, like the prophet Jeremiah, wept and lamented over her. What would you say are the sources of the "pain of God" felt through the history of the chosen people?

The Shepherd, A Shepherdess
(Read Ezekiel 34:11–31)

I myself shall pasture my sheep, I myself shall give them rest—declares the Lord Yahweh. I shall look for the lost one, bring back the stray, bandage the injured and make the sick strong. I shall watch over the fat and healthy. I shall be a true shepherd to them. Ezekiel 34:15–16

WHERE HE PASSED, the scent of animal skin, grass, and moist earth lingered. A breath of star-studded nights, drowsy dawn mists, the brush and murmur of moseying flocks, the pat of a fond hand, a prod of crook, the thump of staff tamping down the path all lasted. He was kindly, quiet, there, full of life, and they caught it. They were other men and women, tenders of sheep, sub-flocks of his, on hills and mountains near him.

The woman who watched her small huddle of wooly birthlings liked him, and fancied she had learned his way. She was feminine, less numerous, steady, and, like him, true. She wore long grass, beads of dew, and the light of moon on her forehead. The hum of shifting sheep and nuzzlings of sleep warmed and cooled her. No matter where, she always heard his whistle. She woke, led, kept, fed, nursed the undergrown, propped, carried the limp, stroked, watered, mothered, cuddled, lavished them into life and lush land. She had long known the shepherd. She knew sheep too, for she was one, in a way, herself.

Good One, I am daughter to your fatherhood, student to your teaching. You have blessed me with life, and I give, as I nurture and wait, that blessing. Let me remember and do that life that I've seen in you.

Questions for Reflection and Discussion

• Ezekiel told of the need for a good shepherd, a reliable leader of Israel. Consider what a disciple is and then describe what a good shepherd would have to impart to a disciple so that she would reliably lead God's people.

• A shepherd(ess) must be alert, confident, quick to respond, and an attentive listener. What would a tender of sheep have to listen to and for? What does a spiritual tender of the flock have to listen to and for?

SUSANNA
(Read Daniel 13)

At midday, when the people had gone away, Susanna would take a walk in her husband's garden. The two elders, who used to watch her every day as she came in to take her walk, gradually began to desire her. Daniel 13:7–8

IT APPEARED that the only tree she had loved under was the tree of life. She was innocent, lovely, delicate. And redeemed.

Death and justice toppled like a felled oak or mastic on her be-
sotted enemies.

God, continue to give me reason to believe that you finally set things
right for the taken, and mistaken, women who nearly die of lies.

QUESTIONS FOR REFLECTION AND DISCUSSION

• Susanna is almost undone by lust and threat and malicious
testimony. In the end, however, she is rescued by truth, after the
protests of a spirit-filled young boy. When stories conflict and
there is a possibility of grave harm, what do you feel is the best
way to get at the truth? What means are available to protect innocent people? Are you yourself more ready to believe a better account of people's conduct, or are you more likely to believe the
worst? Why?

The Bride of Yahweh
(Read Hosea, especially 2:7–25)

I shall betroth you to myself forever,
I shall betroth you in uprightness and justice,
and faithful love and tenderness. Hosea 2:21

THERE WERE PERSISTENT hints that God wanted to marry someone and spend lifetimes hugging their children.

But his tastes were unaccountable. The woman he wanted was the type who would promise her whole soul, make love, and then walk around the block looking for someone else. She was a woman who couldn't quite grasp the idea of totality.

He kept taking her away to deserts. There they reveled in honeymoons and feasts. He would speak to her assuringly, so softly, as the moon rose and ornaments of light spilled from full sky.

She was fine.

And then she would change her mind.

He would be exasperated and then, at a moment's turn, forgive her. And they would begin again.

She herself could not imagine what attracted and kept him. He seemed to see through to something in her soul that she did not even know—some steadiness, some immense capacity, some finally faithful love.

At least when she kissed him she meant it.

He kept silent and kept talking.

Someday she would sit still long enough for him to teach her.

Beloved, my divided heart comes back to you. Heal its cracks, and make me whole.

Questions for Reflection and Discussion

• All of us in some ways fit the description of the "beloved infidel." What is it in us that resists God and the good? How do you account for the human tendency to repeat patterns of sin?

• What practices and resources do you find most helpful in restoring you to grace and rebuilding your resolve to stay close to God? What reassures you of God's endless willingness to forgive?

ON THE DAY OF THE LORD
(Read Joel 2-3)

Blow the ram's horn in Zion!
Order a fast...
assemble the elders,
gather the children,
even infants at the breast! Joel 2:15–16

WHAT WILDNESS would it take? What violent shaking and bloodbath? The clues had always been strong that there would be cataclysms. They startle self-concepts. They shake a worldview. They loosen half-thoughts of God till they jingle and drop.

In the days of Joel they were waiting, too. "Ashes, ashes, all fall down," they childplayed in their timid skin.

The women who sat through the prophet's word believed him: that it would be glad and amazing in the end; that they would dream and see and understand in the aftermath; that the All-Everything would smile and they would stand in a circle of bright Godshine.

But first there was fasting.

And before and after and always there was prayer.

They saw it was more than readying for a wedding or a baby.

It would take persevering, faithful care, and eyes to see past what would look like disaster.

When my whole world, God, comes down, or when the wide earth around me is caught in upheaval and killing, remind me of what I know in my soul: that there are these days of the Lord; that there are also days after.

QUESTIONS FOR REFLECTION AND DISCUSSION

• For Christians, the resurrection of Jesus brings the message that evil and disaster are never the end of the story. What, similarly, in Jewish history indicates that there is always more to come after the apparently unhappy ending?

THE COWS OF BASHAN
(*Read Amos 4:1–3*)

Listen to this..., you cows of Bashan... saying to your husbands, "Bring us something to drink!" Amos 4:1

THERE WERE THOSE WOMEN who lay around wishing that someone would do something so that the kingdom would come.

Father, forgive me, for I have snuggled and eased, gabbed on the phone and watched TV when I should have said, "It's my turn, Lord: send me."

QUESTIONS FOR REFLECTION AND DISCUSSION

• One of the easiest temptations is to fall into the role of the spectator-critic. What are some of the religious and social problems of our day which people typically want "someone" to address but are reluctant to get involved in themselves?

• Cite some examples of women who have become active in combating problems or situations which vexed them. What finally motivated them to personal involvement? In what situations have you found yourself pushed to move from the position of passive observer to that of active proponent of some cause? What got you moving?

THE MOTHER OF PEACE
(Read Micah 4-5; 6:8)

But you (Bethlehem) Ephrathah, the least of the clans of Judah, from you will come for me a future ruler of Israel whose origins go back to the distant past, to the days of old. Micah 5:1

THERE WAS A CHRISTMAS of spirit, a Christmas of thought, generations before there was a child. It was dreamed by the hopers and seers, by the bright flames of life that lit long nights.

Through the mists of their vision, they saw Bethlehem. Perhaps there was the faint flash of the star, a hint broken through from light years off. Perhaps they had, for a moment, a gift of transcending time. It was an event of their prayer.

They saw the form of a mother, the queen of a peaceable kingdom.

Without knowing how or why, they rested their heads for a few seconds on her breast. And they were comforted there for centuries.

I greet, O Heart of Peace, the ever-December, the birth that can be each day with your good word: Shalom. I am glad for our good mother.

QUESTIONS FOR REFLECTION AND DISCUSSION

• Pope John Paul II has often said that the transformation of the world can be accomplished only through the "transformation of the human heart." What inner qualities must people possess to be at peace themselves and to be genuine in the role of peacemaking?

• Micah implies, and Pope Paul VI clearly stated, that justice is the essential prelude to peace. In what specific ways did the Hebrew prophets and Jesus call people to justice?

• How do you account for the centuries of devotion to Mary as Queen of Peace and intercessor for the conversion of the world from violence to mercy? Where does Mary fit into your own involvement in the cause of peace?

THE OLD WOMEN OF NEW JERUSALEM

(Read Zechariah 8:1–17; 9:9–17)

Rejoice heart and soul, daughter of Zion!
Shout for joy, daughter of Jerusalem!
Look, your king is approaching....
He will proclaim peace.... Zechariah 9:9–10

EVEN ON A SHIVER of a day, after wayfaring and ruining through which few remained, a new day might be. A temple could form up from faith and muscle. A people could be pleased to greet one another on the streets of the holy hill. The Jordan and all the rivers flowing to the Dead Sea could take on a mystic, jeweled glitter, and the Dead Sea come to life under skies of glory.

Even yet. Even now, they said.

They were the old women. They were about to turn their walking sticks to shepherd staffs. The children would follow them through the dusty streets. When they would stop at a well, the women would sit. The children would squat around them. The women would tell them what miracles of Israel had been. The women would ask them to notice the one who made them for play and would urge them to learn that most holy and nameless name. They would ask the children to clean and repledge and remake. The women would predict the Messiah-to-be. And the children would promise many fine and good things.

It would be time for headstrong, full-bodied dancing. The old women would clap. They would tap their God-rhythmic feet.

God of the gray sages, let grace go on. May I age in you and teach your sense of timing, so the children may see that from our presents, pasts, and futures, new worlds still dawn.

QUESTIONS FOR REFLECTION AND DISCUSSION

• How can the elderly serve as "bridges" for younger generations, passing on treasured values and traditions and also holding forth future hope and promise? Where are there opportunities in present-day church and society for this to happen?

MESSENGER MALACHI
(Read Malachi)

A message. The word of Yahweh to Israel through Malachi. "I have loved you, says Yahweh. But you ask, 'How have you shown your love?'"
Malachi 1:1–2

"MY MESSENGER," anonymous, untraceable, might well have been a woman. She might have been a hidden brilliance, a genius smuggled into scrolls in men's clothes.

She spoke of love and sin, of propriety and profanation, of the waiting women of Judah and idolatrous wives.

She was reassuring and warning, welcoming and chiding. She was wrapped in love and law.

These were the underpinnings of her message:
- The Lord does not change.
- The unrepentant set fire to themselves and burn.
- The listeners and hangers-on will gambol, hurrah, and parade.
- Lo, Elijah is coming back.
- Thereupon someone even better will arrive: la la!

Lord, you ask for our hearts and minds. Warm mine. Wake me with a heart-to-heart and a thoughtful expectancy. If nothing else, I hope.

QUESTIONS FOR REFLECTION AND DISCUSSION

- The idea that Malachi might have been a woman may be no more than a wild and mistaken guess. However, it is possible to identify some elements of Malachi's prophecy as more feminine in perspective. What, for example?
- While much of Malachi is angry and fiery, where in the prophecy do you find hope and light?

At Last, Elizabeth
(Read Malachi 3:1 and Luke 1:5–25, 44–45)

Elizabeth conceived and for five months she kept to herself, saying, "The Lord has done this for me, now that it has pleased him to take away the humiliation I suffered in public." Luke 1:24–25

WHEN WHOLE TREES snapped, careened against each other, thudded to the ground, and the wind whipped hedgeroot upside down, she felt most at home. When topsoil was long gone, and whole fields cracked, and powder turned the walker's feet gray-beige, she nodded that she knew. The earth was making deserts more than mothers.

For years her prayers had felt like snores, almost saying, quieting down, rising again, then swallowing a sigh. Her meditative timidity—up, down, crescendo, decrescendo, maybe, not, now, no—almost, she thought, but not quite, roused her God, the sleeper. For years she had asked—a blunt, bare beggary.

One night after the man had spent a strange spell in the temple, rain fell. The wind stood still. She almost drowned in garden. It would be a son.

The old, old father was as one whose mouth had been burned shut with sealing wax, though he had had, and still had, his own fire.

No matter. For the time she sang enough for two of them.

She flowered.

God, I am thanksgiver. In my own time you have given me, me too, surprise.

QUESTIONS FOR REFLECTION AND DISCUSSION

• With which of the foremothers does Elizabeth have much in common? And, among his forebears, whose conception parallels that of her son?

• Elizabeth, Zechariah, Joseph, and Mary were among the anawim, the faithful and impoverished remnant among whom the Messiah would come. How does Elizabeth represent the poor in spirit?

Mary, The Girl of Nazareth

(Read Luke 1:26–38)

In the sixth month the angel Gabriel was sent by God to a town in Galilee called Nazareth, to a virgin betrothed to a man named Joseph, of the House of David… Luke 1:26–27

IT WAS EARLY and happy. Layer of light added upon last layers of night, and so the world was opening into day.

For the moment she was afraid. Even though the being of light in his tender, bright manform had told her in the kindest voice not to be. She knew of the years of hope and the years of fracturing. She had learned of the times of glory and the ages of decay.

She knew, had learned, but was too young, too good, to understand promises made and then choked back. She was taken off guard. She did her best as she replied. It was an attempt at concentration, a leap into blinding light.

There was God and more in her heart. It seemed enough.

And so she was ready for someone releasing and God-sent and timeless to come. It surpassed all wishing. It made word flesh. Yes, she would; of course, he could. Even if....Yes.

Hail Mary, full of grace, let me, let all women be, one, for all, over and over, Christbearer, bringer of light, speaker of peace, mother of magnificent possibility. And so we begin again...with an "O!"...reverently. Amen.

QUESTIONS FOR REFLECTION AND DISCUSSION

• Purity of heart and belief in God's promise were part of what made Mary's consent so ready and so possible. As a channel of grace, she has been described as transparent. She has also been called a spouse of the Holy Spirit. What do you see in Mary that inspires you and gives you a sense of what you can do in cooperation with God?

• How does the "yes" of Mary inaugurate a new Genesis?

242
Sm63
#C7665   Smith, Pamela.

AUTHOR
Woman Story: Biblical models

TITLE
for our time.

242
Sm63
#C7665

Smith, Pamela.

Woman story: Biblical models for our time.